Kinda Keats

KINDA KEATS

POEMS ON KEATS HOUSE

DEBORAH TYLER-BENNETT

Shoestring Press

All rights reserved. No part of this work covered by the copyright hereon may be reproduced or used in any means – graphic, electronic, or mechanical, including copying, recording, taping, or information storage and retrieval systems – without written permission of the publisher.

Printed by imprintdigital
Upton Pyne, Exeter
www.imprintdigital.net

Typeset by Narrator
www.narrator.me.uk
enquiries@narrator.me.uk

Published by Shoestring Press
19 Devonshire Avenue, Beeston, Nottingham, NG9 1BS
(0115) 925 1827
www.shoestringpress.co.uk

First published 2013
© Copyright: Deborah Tyler-Bennett

The moral right of the author has been asserted.

ISBN 978 1 907356 90 2

ACKNOWLEDGEMENTS

These poems were largely written as result of being a *Poetry Lives Here* Resident Writer at Keats House, Hampstead, in the summer of 2010. This involved writing in the house, delivering workshops, talking to visitors and fellow writers, and exploring both the objects and settings of some of Keats's life. 'Ghost Writing' is also part of a longer sequence of poems, *The Ladies of Harris's List*.

Versions of these poems first appeared in *Writ in Water* (City of London: Keats House, 2011), *Here We go Round the Mulberry Tree*, (City of London: Keats House, 2013), *Poetry Salzburg* (Austria), *The Raintown Review* (US), *London Grip* (online), *The Kinks in Literature* (online) and *Poetry Scotland*.

'On looking into a picture of Keats's Death Mask in the Observer', was (under a slightly different title) my first published poem on Keats, in *Angel Exhaust* back in 1997, so I wanted to include a new, post Keats House, version of it here.

Thanks are due to John Lucas and all at Shoestring Press and Narrator, Jan Pimblett and Maureen Roberts, Nick Field, Martyn Bennett, my family, the late Jack Yates, Alison Jacques, and all the staff at Keats House who made me so welcome. Thanks also to Sally and Ian King for letting me try out some of the poems at the *Callander Poetry Weekend*, and to all the writers/ audience members who heard versions of the poems, particularly at the *Keats Festivals* 2010/ 2011 (Keats House).

See www.cityoflondon.gov.uk/keatshousehampstead

For everyone at Keats House

CONTENTS

Prelude	**1**
Keats's Magic Coat	3
On looking into a picture of Keats's Death Mask	4
Inside/Outside	**5**
Keats Grove Ode: Hide and Seek	7
Keats Grove Ode II: Ghosts by Daylight	9
Briefest Encounters	10
Still Life with Radical Spirits	11
John and Fanny	12
John and Tonic	13
This House, Your Heart	**15**
Self Reflection in Regency Looking-Glass	17
Fanny Brawne's Dressing-Room	18
Two Sonnets	20
Moonlight at Sea, Dark on Board	22
Two Masks	23
Kinda Keats	**25**
Numerous as Shadows… Haunting Fairly…	27
Kinda Keats	29
Points Failure	30
Great Escapes	32
Line	33
Ghost Writing	35
Heath Hurst	37
Self, Dissolving	38
Housing 'Junkets'	39
Notes to individual poems	40

Prelude

That you would give me gloves of the skin of a fish...
That you would give me shoes of the skin of a bird...
('Donal Og', Irish, 8th-Century)

KEATS'S MAGIC COAT

Depending how viewed, poet standing robed,
projecting lantern slides, unlikely coat.
Buttons blink from acorns to ducks' eyes
to spangled poppy-heads, their troubled dreaming.

Lapels: kingfisher flash; fresh-moulted hen feathers.
Fabric: stiff white wastes old Gods grumble in;
then, just as sudden, misted Autumn's
russet-apple skin.

Let's not wax too poetic.

Garment soon stale soaked as poverty, thin-
lining sewer splashed, sweating Peterloo's spilt blood,
that story dark as Newgate's Knocker.
On misrule's days apes Mr Brummell's
finery, quick turned
                      pauper grave clothes.

Most moments

self same coat cloud-wraps.

Him, shadow stepping visitor to his house.
Consider, as waters fill your eye,
words fluttering poet's mouth
settle on the coat
                inscribing moths
'John' re-fleshed by their tangle-hearted lace.

ON LOOKING INTO A PICTURE OF KEATS'S DEATH MASK

in the *Observer*

I.

Set features flash news-print –
shoved by shock's obsidian hand I plunge
depths, dodging a sunk hull's rib.

Plaster mask, underwater statue.

II.

Emerge gasping at still warm death,
sea-beet's pages creaking to the touch
before they're cut.

Did Keats see his life circling like pictures in a zoetrope
as he lay perspiring? Perhaps his last ship's darkened cabin,
fretful faces, jig of words from poems he'd never write.

III.

Fold newsprint, crack the image,
lightning limning waves.

Merman face – lined mouth
sea-holly's interlacing veins.

Inside/Outside

KEATS GROVE ODE: HIDE AND SEEK

(For Jan Pimblett and Maureen Roberts)

Crack on Brown's clock-face, rain-drop's line
uncertain moment blurring time.

Keats tired of bed,
from sofa viewed passing trade.

Now, I scan self-same street's
well-versed game, its Hide and Seek.
Visitors chorus room to room,
garden, actor – Keats,
moleskin wash of copper leaves.
Woman's firebrand hair
a sunflower. So far
no gypsies after hare skins,
'un-presuming bonnets' of old women…

Rather this walnut fisted, buggied toddler;
baby in bee-stripes bumbling across lawns,
actor trying lines on her; a spaniel
looks as if knowing the score;
silvered *Allegra* fins past,
driver's coolest *Ray Bans*.

Not harebell skirts, damped muslins,
(*Dolce and Gabana* gypsy splendour,
faux hare-fur jerkins.)

Skittering cabbage white proceeds
girl in tortoise-shell silk, heading for *Summer
Bargains*. John's sometime lover?
Eyes scavenging house,

quickest smile, then gone.
His gaze waiting her return all afternoon.

Private Hide and Seek
                        framed by my gate

conjured gap between stanzas.

KEATS GROVE ODE II: GHOSTS BY DAYLIGHT

Brown's study window hardens against July afternoon,
leaves reflecting velvety as parlour-curtains,
girls navigate the house, penny-plain
Fanny Brawne and Fanny Keats.

John felt his sister trail mapped streets,
wraith-like. Blanched as his Knight-at-arms
sensed himself 'posthumous' while alive.

This afternoon strays, trick of watered light,
ladybird's blobbed wax on my writing hand,
below mulberry, fruits' spilled claret.

I'd like to think him here, webbed gently in
(like Shelley, non-belief won't go for it).
Still, as I tread the back-door path
in tightened grass, thrush feather, trapped,
his sort of beauty.

This lovely world comes at a grim fixed-price,
left poems and letters always point that way,
under conservatory roofs a cabbage-white
batters its frayed wings against unyielding glass.

BRIEFEST ENCOUNTERS

Poet on sabre-legged seat,
concentrates.
Screws up paper, throws
corner-wards.

Face toward you,
journeying realms new.
Look, rippled thought.
If spoken to, would he reply?

Flickering his mind's eye,
word un-coming,
moment near,
from mulberry, blackbird's clarion.

Visitors (distant
time, another space)

shadow spirits thrown
by truly magic lanterns.

STILL LIFE WITH RADICAL SPIRITS

Lay down rouged hearts, jet aces, lacy jacks
on this cool basement's dining table,
wine dregs metallic at throat's back,
shucked oysters, rock-pool in a pewter dish

fit for Severn's pencil, Haydon's line,
not Pavilion feast but literary supper –
cherry brandy, coarse bread, chestnuts
firing mouths like angry-mob dissension.

Outdoors, usual knaves rule London's gaming,
carriage-wheels spattering beggar, vendor, medic.
John's sweetheart will be queen among
spades patterning Hampstead's iron-work.

Lay down lace hearts, rouge aces, and jet jacks,
Leigh Hunt's *Examiner* put by – Prince enraged
at maverick pages, editor consigned to
prison-rooms bowered with trellis-roses

there hearing erection of the gallows (one
warder taking him to roofs with promised view
of fields, to look down on a *Tom Putt* featured girl
about to hang there for her infant's killing).

Cell made comfortable, liberty a lost
turn around the Heath, supper with friends,
then coat put on to go, as they laid down
newsprint aces, inky jacks, their bloodied hearts.

JOHN AND FANNY

> *'This is the gift it comes at a price...'* Florence and the Machine, *'Rabbit Heart'*.

Framing window's grid, balustrades'
rakish balance. Claimed bench
beneath chanting leaves,
tall London-plane.
                        Young couple –
Laughing, wrangling, joking love
for *You Tube,* mobile, *Facebook.*

Briefest afternoon's comparisons:
Slender ankle; *Converse* laden foot;
freckles shaded under his
baseball-cap (*NYC,* city un-witnessed).

She make believes to slap,
they break apart... Then kiss...

Such memories, with other costume
Keats might have had in Italy,
recalled smile, pout, tenderest slap,
but not bearing to think on these too long –

Clouded hair's inked cumulus
cold blots last summer's sun.

JOHN AND TONIC

Tonight, as John Hegley sang poems, him coaxing,
Keats House chorusing (happily, scarily, uproariously)
bright green parakeet, g-and-t's slice of lime,
bounced into trees with tomato-billed, fractious mate.

Readers… audience digging ribs: 'Did you see?'
Unconcerned, his own deft poetry
dainty-clawed parakeet hung upside down,
mate off, soaring.

Passing gilt Music Room as I was leaving
saw through framing windows, beaming
faces, their interior candles. Gazing
netted trees, caught love bird laughter.

This House, Your Heart

SELF REFLECTION IN REGENCY LOOKING-GLASS

'You either see it or you don't'...
Dennis Severs creator of 18 Folgate Street, Spitalfields

Breath-misted mercury, emergent foil clouds.
See yourself ebonised shadow figure
donning habit of former times.
                                      Behind your outline,
window glass (*faux* raindrops or sheeted downpour
considered, now, imperfections), blown
garden's backdrop, sea-trees thrashing your
silhouette's rock, its citadel.
Smoked picture masks
face, hands, dress.

Hypnotic glass's tidal wash,
light loiters, fractures, scatters…
Far off room's clock chimes…
House holding tight.

Uncertain century, ticks echo,
bristles flay stone just beyond sight,
likewise, scratching pen. Then
someone steps into the room, goes out again –

You turn, space emptying,
                          speak his familiar name.

FANNY BRAWNE'S DRESSING-ROOM

These rooms will stay, certainly.
Just in case, commit to memory.

Place changes, seemingly secure,
tenanted space become unsure.

'You never know,' takes over, gleamed
lurid opiate dream.

Fashion albums playing host
to 'group of well known dandies' ghosts:

Rakes, Fops, Cyprians,
evolving as Victorians.

And I could stay here all gilt afternoon,
re-animate sartorial chameleons. Soon

dusked walls make sunshine memory
and, wondering if rooms will stay

means listing objects, mind's-eye inventory,
of chintzy papers, dresser's mahogany,

windows, knobs, and door-frames,
covers, cupboards, mirrors, keys,

gown graced albums, photographs,
while, from the garden, floating laughter…

Below, Byron's lamp, terracotta shell
transformed by acolyte to ink well,

snap of Fanny's post-John life,
(muse as someone else's wife)

scribbled margins, ring's almandine sheen,
senses restoring letters, pen-knives, treen,

and on a boat, sick exiles did the same
for house-bound objects, home-moored names.

TWO SONNETS

Keats's Bedroom

Hardest to be here, near his bed,
pen-and-wash light of this slight room.
Visiting Severn's death-sketch, webbed
ink suggesting 'wake him'. Catacomb's
stark day-lily, poet's white-mask shakes
as if the sickly, living, John's still here,
gaze flickered-insect caught in lace,
'do stay' he whispers. There's a moth tear
on his night-shirt, I consider comic
stories for him, tales of friends,
some diversion from this chronic
silence, thinking moth-holes won't mend,
stare at his shirt. 'Better now... You go...'

Young smile's flame gutters from view.

The Sofa Bed

House's oasis, sofa's lizard-green,
healing, calm, solitary
as if trapped by jet iron-work, screening
borders. Wayfarers come, and mulberry
afternoons are run, children laughing
all reddle-handed, raiding fruits,
shadowed marionettes on grass,
tiniest jiving, stomping fat jelly-boots.
Poet's sofa, primed for watching play,
waiting single sight of Fanny Brawne,
from 'pleasant prison'… Only yesterday…

 A nearby bar, and Van Morrison's thrawn
gravel vocals, song of love and hurt,
arterial mulberry stains a cambric-shirt.

MOONLIGHT AT SEA, DARK ON BOARD

Coasts seeming clear, Hogarth's lightning strikes,
momentary panic, squalling crowds. Worst things
happen when closing doors, strolling off, *Rake's
Progress* got it right. Crunching path
heard again only when dreaming.

Quitting home, John's senses reeling…
Left friends. Love's locking face. No picture.
She'd gifted him a white cornelian,
later turned in fevered palm… Looped hair
swirling laudanum-free nightmare.

Maria Crowther docked before setting off,
shadow-self bridled, hell-bent for *Wentworth Place*.
Brown's Hogarth collection riotous – haunting
as *Guy's* Admittance Hall, London's whoring.

On board, sopped planks, fellow consumptives,
unwelcome memories: papered walls; sofa's
plump green; framing his girl, a shapely window,
fond notes penned for under his pillow.

Dissolving hearth-scape, vanished calm,
cornelian fretting spent man's palm.

TWO MASKS

Night, day,
gasped life, surest death,
or, if cliché,
one rubbed coin's sides.

John's *Life Mask* says its piece –
Behold our Man, thriving, striving,
cream-ware skin betraying
work worries. Moth-flickering
mouth begs students ask
how was he masked, un-masked?

Features bound by lint then plaster,
straws up nostrils, sharpest on the tongue,
world piling, austere
ice-burial. Long
wait. Mask removed.
Artist's hands tremulous, face below
re-birthed, re-cleansed, quite new.

Death Mask clamours –
Students call:
'Mum, Dad, lost them all;
his Brother… Man, that's everyone!'
History's after-shocks,
George's emigration,
works unsold, cold counted costs…
Unjust pages, piercing reviews,
'Hard facing him for long,
as if he knows you knew':

I seem books you started, never finishing,
mine name writ on water.
I'm Love's strange vocal. Un-diminishing
my tender-hearted page.

Leaving, young writers seeking sun.
From plane-tree, thrush's fractured song
carries eagle-hearted, over London.

Kinda Keats

NUMEROUS AS SHADOWS… HAUNTING FAIRLY…

(For Nick Field and everyone at Keats House)

I.

Visitor's Book's automatic writing, school
workshops' graffitied sheets,
tell him all sorts, found poems,
miniature confidences.

Americans 'do' the house,
sprint by me. Two women from Spain
ponder: 'Girlfriend … Sister, single Christian name.'
'What's a Greek urn?' (Style of Eric Morecambe,
always one).
'Short, so what? Still handsome'
says a girl: 'I'd date him.'
Lingering teens love pages with the passion
my Aunt reserved for Byron,
me for David Essex.

II.

Down the road, Hampstead's lit faces:
flambéd beards so long. Son,
his equally grizzled Dad stand, Blakean;
Tramp's coat, autumn leafy,
secrets in calcified bag, not potted Basil;
Dapper drunk careering Heath edge
all sixties pop star –
Mod badges, feathered Fedora, pinstripe flash.

On wildest Heath,
(getting lost distinctest possibility)
flesh gone, charry
willow-stick through scooped body,
dead hedgehog staked.

III.

Fanny Brawne's fashionistas, rocking
Well Walk, wax elegant. Dandies
come to Spa, sneer, gallantry masking
up-manship, mocking Byronics here-abouts,
flamboyance *sans* price tag doesn't count.

IV.

Back to the house… its crowds,
one mob waking John with nightmares,
Hogarth print of rabid dissenters
(Brown purchased for sketching from)
satires on credulity, gulled into buying tales
of devil-smirched girls giving birth to leverets,
grim preachers lusting, gurning cherubs.

Scoffers, canting jibers… Maybe reviewers,
only recalled connected to his name, howling,
baying, jabbering, hell-hound throng,

Poetry's heels snapped *en-route* to Critics' Bedlam.

V.

House used to be darker. Pictures askew.
Not new-build curators say he knew.
I cleaned here years, then stopped, now come
again. Fresh colours, special, sort of gets to you.

KINDA KEATS

'See here it is – I hold it towards you.'
(John Keats, 'This Living Hand, Now Warm and Capable')

For Ray Davies

Keats House reveals time's glitchery again,
half day's workshop over in a hand-stretch.
Now, outside the *Euphorium Café*
we're sipping coffee,
watching passers-by skirting the Heath
in sudden heat.
'Time swallowing happens here,' you say,
'expect the unexpected.'

As if to illustrate, there's Ray
Davies from *The Kinks*, sentinel
by unlikeliest orange van…

… We laugh, Ray Davies on a sunny afternoon.

Keats's friend, Haydon, could have thumbnail sketched
songwriter's sun-cut silhouette, us soon
turned to *clafoutis aux cerises*, bitter-
cocoa torte, and *latte*… crumbs of this Hampstead
summer almanac.

While, at Keats House, as clocks go winding back,
an orange van steals by. As lovers stand
for photos against Keats's mulberry,
the poet stretches out his, tenderest, hand.

POINTS FAILURE

> *He caught a cold in the Island of Mull… and the Physician here
> (Inverness) thinks him too thin and fevered to proceed on our journey…'*
> Keats's friend, Charles Brown, 1818

For Sally and Ian King

Ten minutes… Lose connection for Stirling?
Half-hour's wait, if so. Whimpering pup at the carriage-
back, baby's squeaker mimics chew-toy.

Thoughts of Brown and Keats's
Celtic sojourn, their sodden return,
human baggage on coach-tops or
pressed between a fugged interior's
strangers, woollens steaming.
Burdensome, that medical training,
identifying rashes, fevers, goutish shifting.

Now coastal-bluffs come glossed by train-
windows, barley-stooks clipped-
coin bright before sluggish rain.
Soundtrack – droplets' applause,
passengers eased, not hirpled through squalls.

                      Points failure's
wait… ten tetchy minutes inconvenience.

No feet testing boggy passes, mossed-
trees figured for tweed-backed poachers.
Trying friendship, hope, deep love of Burns,
thankful for inn doors' faint glow-worms.

      Ten minutes.

Fraction more. Off again.
Sitting pretty Edinburgh bound,
I hear that holiday settling on his chest, coughing
agitating him and mindful Brown –

Points failure – dispensed with these ten minutes, less, is nothing.

GREAT ESCAPES

For Mum and Dad

"*And with thee fade away into the forest dim…*"

Bed-ridden, badly off painter, stubby tubes hand-me-down
as coats Grandma passed on to his wife. Other peoples'
colours dictating subjects, moods… Richer artists' off-cuts
sometimes gifting hardboard, lumpy palettes. Still, when
fired he'd paint on cushions, chair-backs, table covers.
Sale meaning full tubes toward the next – cherished
whites, or brushes fresh from crackling paper, not clarted with
another's paint. Gran bought her chosen canvas, 'Bluebell
Wood', regretting one 'he couldn't bring himself to part with' –
'Gypsy Encampment' fashioned from glutted red: dancers;
firelight; smoking Rom; reluctant horse; encased within
necessity's thinned light. Unvarnished, warming means-
tested parlour more than their sparsest range. His name?
Evaporated mist. 'Bluebell Wood' summering Mum's wall,
reversed sky of forest floor, paint exploring where, for years,
he hadn't walked. Brush-strokes, eked sun loitering oak,
ash, elm. Poor bloke's bluebell carpet, so right you hear
wood pigeon   raven   distant shot
mole-eyed miners seeking 'summat fresh' for Sunday's pot.

LINE

'As if he himself felt the cut' Benjamin Robert Haydon, 1814, *of an executioner sketched from Titian's Death of Saint Peter the Martyr.*

I.

Plaster cast – *Something* classical
Maenad, Fury, purchased *somewhere other*,
charms fast *fading*, like a one-night stand,
Haydon *wants* it in the bigger picture.
Not for him *Chinoiserie,*
bluebell Ho-Ho birds, fondant fancies, *but*
ancient scenes, Maenads, or something Biblical. *Fury*
besting his kinder self, *haunts Haydon.*

Sketches aged best. How *he would* hate it!
Sitters' *want,* their desperation,
the much-mired *honesty of*
a murderer with a face sublime,
blasé, indifferent to the framing noose, succeeds.

They'd inhabit *any* street.
Just swap their linens for a logo-heavy T.
Redeeming light can't make
their *truths less granite-edged.*

II.

*Something
somewhere other,
fading,
wants
Chinoiserie,
but
fury
haunts Haydon.
He would
want
the honesty of
a Murderer with a face sublime…
Blasé… Indifferent …*

*Any
just
redeeming light can't make
truths less granite-edged.*

GHOST WRITING

'Rain would not have kept them away twenty-six years ago' B R Haydon, 1846.

Panoramas of new London eddying past
legends diamond-scratched on rippled glass,
lost hoardings flicker glazed-brick shops,
gone incumbents shadow Paddington Old Church.

City story's refusal to lie down, not recorded ghost
but ought to be. Benjamin Robert Haydon, gruff
romantic, fails to shoot himself, slitting throat
within his oil stained studio. It's 1846,

stalked by disappointment, outliving
loving friends. Recalling Keats
(more haunted by un-sold canvases, slope-
spined spectres in back rooms, warehouses …

Lazarus lurks Mountfields' Upholsterers,
Crucifixion's in a Lisson Grove hayloft).
Haydon's life bumps in the night,
half-open doorway capturing

frenzied last of him,
eyes rabid with untaken roads,
fame stepping back through windows
shuttered against June's deluge.

Biblical scenes unfashionable in heartbeats,
commission for decorating Parliament denied. At sixty,
self promotion rattling the Egyptian Hall,
paintings form sweated patches by day's end.

It rains, booked rooms stay empty, along the way
Piccadilly clamours to view General Tom Thumb,
his epic smallness.

Angels' yew-tree wings from Paddington
imply full stops, ends, exclamation marks…
Something undying catches on close winds…

Clicking latch as Haydon's studio opens, foot-steps echoing,
brushes examined… bills, and Bailiff's letters flung…

Soft coat's billowing – eddying crowds got-up to see Tom Thumb.

HEATH HURST

'No change' I say. By time knowing this wrong
he's gone, walked on...
                              Face, imprinted for me,
waxy imprint of a tassie...

Euphorium Café lunch-hour ticks.
He's back. Iron-
work hair, abject stare,
agate teeth, ex-resident
cobwebby in heat-haze.

Illumined at tables where Lamia,
Madeline, Isabella nestle
near cup-cakes...
Streamed motes transform his face,
young Porphyro.

Seems we seldom know
ghosts near,
haunts his corner... wavers...
disappears...
Street sign's stylish tiles spell
enigmatic name, once his:
                              HEATH HURST.

SELF, DISSOLVING

Which am I? Not so much *Jasper-Ware* plaques
   mythologizing life's events. Pretty
      posthumous-prints, improbable, imagine fey-limbed boy
         encountering bare-knuckled city!

      Haydon and Severn caught me
         (sketch both's metier, though neither'd own it).
            Which am I? Take harder look, eyes have it?
            Something waylaid sidles past.

            Imposing truths: Deathly life masks.

         What of silhouettes, scarring
         plain ground as poems scar?
         Brown cut, pasted, corked features,
         cravat's *Don Juan* edge, its lava-cameo.

         Fill colours as you go.

               Which am I? Sawdust muffled street ballads,
                  hooves not engines. Across the *Heath,* gypsies arguing
                  the toss, brick-maker, pot boy, and the ladies, lap-
                  dog snappery, spun-lace fears.

      Shadow-puppetry, candle's winding-
         sheet, misted choleric Thames,
      thumb smudge, breath vaporising
   glass, oiled palms imprinting balustrade.

         I'm ink, encountering pristine page.

HOUSING 'JUNKETS'

Keats's Cabinet of Curiosity – I place
his sighs and longings, keep them safe:
wild trudges; Scottish coach's bone-shook way;
scrubbed notes from lectures on anatomy;
cherry-ace heart fronting a playing-card;
lonely schoolboy crossing mud-carked yards.

Bad memory knocking varnished wood, rebelling,
silhouette comes bitter-jet as keening,
face young and clammy figuring off oysters,
fingers reach for water-logged dog roses.
One drawer's greased by chop-house meagre food
another's an incision drawing blood.

Best shutting both, likewise third along,
leery with a drunkard's slurry song,
one chortles nick-name, 'Junkets,'
the next, judicial: 'Well, then, Mr Keats?'
Thames water drips from foliate name-plate
hinges rusting with his voice: 'too late
for me, the critics' turn, too late!'

Junkets cabinet, let Leigh Hunt place
night-picked garlands, roped with poor man's lace.

NOTES TO INDIVIDUAL POEMS

For biographical details see Motion, Andrew, *John Keats* (London: Faber and Faber, 1997).

Prelude

Keats's Magic Coat: *'Donal Og', Eighth-century Irish Gaelic poem, translated and adapted by Lady Augusta Gregory/ Newgate phrase from a taxi driver en-route to Keats House.*

Inside/Outside

Keats Grove Ode I: *Lines on gypsies and old women taken from Keats's letter to his sister, Fanny, 8th Feb, 1820, copy in his friend, Brown's, Study, Keats House.* Keats Grove Ode II: *Keats letters to Brown (1820) speak of himself and his siblings as ghost-like. Poem title from Keats's words on-board the Maria Crowther in 1820, (Motion, 541).* Still Life with Radical Spirits: *Written as a result of the workshop with Gifted and Talented Students at Keats House, 8, 07, 2010. Tom Putt is a traditional English apple.*

This House, Your Heart

John and Fanny: *Florence and the Machine, 'Rabbit Heart', Lungs, Island Records, 2009. Quote at beginning of* 'Self Reflection in Regency Looking-Glass': *Dennis Severs, 18 Folgate Street: The Tale of A House in Spitalfields (London: Chatto and Windus, 2001), 1. This house, your heart is also adapted from a Severs phrase.* Fanny Brawne's Dressing Room: *Cyprians – Courtesans.* Moonlight at Sea, Dark on Board: *Title words from Joseph Severn's sketch of the Maria Crowther, reproduced on the upstairs wall near Keats's bedroom/ Images from Hogarth prints taken from engravings at Keats House.* Two Masks: *Written as a result of Gifted and Talented Workshops, Keats House (8-9/ 07/ 2010).*

Kinda Keats

Numerous as Shadows…: *Title from John Keats 'The Eve of Saint Agnes', (1820) and words at the poem's end written after talking to the Keats House cleaning staff.* Kinda Keats: *Title adapted from The Kinks' album, Kinda Kinks (1965)/ 'This Living Hand…' quotation in Keats at Wentworth Place (London: Borough of Camden, 1971), 63.* Points Failure: *Quotation in Motion, 295.* Great Escapes: *See Keats at Wentworth Place, 47.* Line: *See Haydon, 1786-1846, Royal Albert Memorial Museum, 1986, 3, of an executioner sketched from Titian's Death of Saint Peter the Martyr.* Ghost Writing: *Haydon's 1846 journal entry in Old and New London (Edward Walford, London: Cassell, Vol 5, 1881), 209.* Self, Dissolving: *In 1819 Keats wrote to Fanny Brawne that he felt himself to be 'dissolving' (Motion, 470).* Housing 'Junkets': *'Junkets' was Hunt's nickname for Keats, see Anthony Holden The Wit in the Dungeon: A Life of Leigh Hunt (London: Little Brown, 2005), 111.*